Family HISTORY

BHOLA KASHYAP

Family HISTORY

BHOLA KASHYAP

authorHOUSE®

AuthorHouse™
1663 Liberty Drive
Bloomington, IN 47403
www.authorhouse.com
Phone: 833-262-8899

Published by AuthorHouse 07/19/2024

ISBN: 979-8-8230-2964-3 (sc)
ISBN: 979-8-8230-2963-6 (e)

Library of Congress Control Number: 2024913506

Print information available on the last page.

Any people depicted in stock imagery provided by Getty Images are models,
and such images are being used for illustrative purposes only.
Certain stock imagery © Getty Images.

This book is printed on acid-free paper.

Tameva Mata cha pita tameva,
Tamewa bandhu cha sakha tameva,
Tameva vidya draviram tameva
Tameva sarvam mammam deva deva.

Dedication

This Book is dedicated to my Mother,
Father & the entire loving family.

I would not have been able to become the person that I am today if it wasn't for my *mom*. She was the embodiment of strength, real confidence, determination, and courage. She is my real hero. Observing her confidently and positively sail through the tough times further increased my admiration and love for her. I know she is showering her blessings from heaven on my family and me.

Mom, I love you and miss you.
   – Bhola Kashyap

Shri Phulchand Sahu Jee ka Family Introduction

Death Year (1911)

Your Grandfather (Dada Jee), his name was Hori Sahu. Under his care you grew up in Sasaram. Sasaram once belonged to Sahabad District then it became a District itself later on. It is now called Sasaram District of State Bihar. Your Father's name (Hori Sahu's father) was Jaggu Sahu and your mother's name was Marhachia Sahun. Your father belongs to Sasaram. He left Sasaram and went to Kutumba to search for better living & earning opportunities. Kutumba is now under Aurangabad District, before it was previously under Gaya District of State Bihar. He started making good living through short spanned business & farming and took care of Family very well.

Family History Names

Shri Hori Sahu & Name Unknown
Kutumba, Aurangabad.
His Father is Jaggu Sahu.
Shri Prayag Sahu wife Smt Ramdei Sahun
Shri Jaggu Sahu & Shrimati Merhachia Sahun
Shri Phulchand Sahu (Exp.1911) & Shrimati Yamuna Devi
Shri Bhikhari Sahu – Wife: Kaga Sahun
Shrimati Lakeshri Devi Married to Sri,
Chhathu Sahu (Kutumba) Aurangabad,

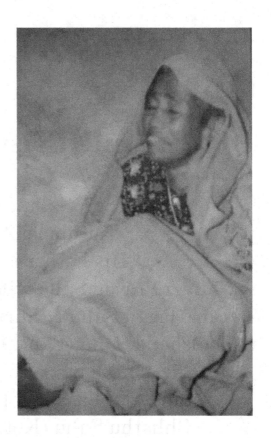

Bhikhari Sahu   *Kaga Devi*

Lakeshri Devi wife of Chhathu Shu

Introduction of Bhikhari Sahu Family

Shri, Bhikahari Sahu & Shrimati, Wife: Kaga Sahun
Kaga Sahun's father's name is Dukhan Sahu.
Village Chainpur, 2 km away from Daltongunj, Palamu.
Married have following Children:

Sons: 3
1. Hira Lal Kashyap
2. Shri Moti Chand Kashyap
3. Shri, Ram Chandra Kashyap

Daughters: 3
1. Shrimati Samudri Devi
2. Murthi Devi
3. Shrimati Panpati Devi

Late Ramdei Sahun Born 15th 1915 to July 27th 199
Wife of Late Prayag Sahu 4th March 1947
Banka - Jharkhand India
Own Children Born All in Banka
Mrs. Gangajal Devi   Mrs. Yashoda Devi
Mrs. Pavitri Devi   Mrs. Laxmi Devi
Mrs. Parvati Devi   Mrs. Kawalpati Devi
          Dr. Banshi P. Kashyap MD
          Dr. Bhola P. Kashyap MD

Shrimati Ramdei Sahun

Introduction of Shri Prayag Sah and Shrimati Ramdei Sahun

Shri Prayag Sahu (Kutumba) and
Shrimati Ramdei Sahun (Garhwa) married
and had the following Children:

Sons: 2
1. Dr. Banshi P Kashyap
2. Dr. Bhola P Kashyap

Daughters: 6
1. Shrimati, Gangagal Devi- Married to Shiv Shanker Sahu
2. Shrimati Pavitri Devi- Lallu Sahu
3. Shrimati, Yashoda Devi- Ram Lagan Sahu
4. Shrimati, Parvati Devi- Prabhu Sahu
5. Shrimati Laxmina Devi- Raja Ram Kashyap
6. Shrimati Kawalpati Devi- Jagdish Prasad Kashyap

Banka House Picture

Bhola Kashyap

Bullock cart attach with farming history

Banka House Picture

Shri Prayag Sahu (Kutumba) and Shrimati Ramdei Sahun(Garhwa) married and had the following Children:

Shrimati Ramdei Sahun

Dr. Bhola Kashyap and
Dr. Banshi Kashyap

Parwati Devi, Pavitri Devi, Gangajal Devi,Yashoda Devi,
Kawalpati Devi, Laxmina Devi

Introduction of Shrimati Gangajal Devi & Shri, Shiv shanker Sahu

GangaJal Devi & Shiv Shanker Sahu
s/o Bhuneshwer Sahu from Garhwa,
Jha(Bihar) had the following Children:

Daughters: 3
1. Gulabi Devi
2. Sushila Devi
3. Pratima Devi

Sons: 3
1. Ramjee Prasad Kashyap
2. Suresh Prasad Kashyap
3. Subhash Kashyap

Introduction Of Shrimati, Pavitri Devi and Shri Lallu Sahu -HazariBaugh

Shrimati Pavitri Devi and Lallu Sahu-Hazaribagh

Son: 3
1. Umesh Kashyap
2. Mahendra Kashyap
3. Sanjay Kashyap

Daughter: 1
1. Rima Devi

Introduction of Shrimati,Yashoda Devi & Shri Ram Lagan Sahu- LesliGunj

Yashoda Devi & Ram Lagan
Sahu- Lesligunj-Palamu

Sons: 2
1. Gopal Pd Kashyap
2. Ramadhar Pd. Kashyap

Daughter: 3
1. Nirmala Devi
2. Shradha Devi
3. Madhuri Devi

Introduction of Shrimati, Parvati Devi & Shri,Prabhu Sahu-Kutumba-Aurangabad, Bihar

Daughter: 2
1. Shushila Devi
2. Shusma Devi

Introduction of Shrimati Laxmina Devi and Shri, Raja Ram Kashyap-Sasaram-Ranchi.

Laxmina Devi-Rajaram Kashyap-Ranchi

Daughter: 1
1. Poonam Kashyap

Son: 3
1. Arvind Kashyap
2. Arun Kr Kashyap
3. Abhay Kr Kashyap

Introduction of Shrimati Kawalpati Devi and Sri, - Jagdish Prasad Kashyap- Japla- Garhwa.

Kawalpati Devi-Jagdish Prasad Kashyap-Garhwa

Son: 1
1. Vinod Kr Kashyap

Daughter: 1
1. Sujata Devi

Introduction of Sri,Bhikhari Sahu and Sri Prayag Sahu-Kutumba-Banka and Shrimati Yamuna Devi

Bhikhari Sahu & Prayag Sahu moved from Kutumba to Banka, Meral Block, Garhwa Jharkhand along with Yamuna Devi wife of Phool Chand Sahu. After the death of Phoolchand Suhu in 1911, they could not tolerate the Grief & sadness. They stayed in Kutumba for two years after that they moved to Banka in 1912-13. Smt, Yamuna Devi was very instrumental in establishing the business in a small Village, She was such a nice lady everyone around her was inspired with her behavior & nature.

Bhikhari Sahu was only 11 year old & Pryag Sahu help in the business. They started small business in Banka. They established good Business in short span of time with hard work. Yamuna Devi was very smart business lady with good nature and kind to other people. It cannot be described in word, still people has not forgotten what she has done during that time. They acquired about 500 acres of land in seven villages. Became a land lord, during that time there was king-Ship or,

(Land-lordship) in India. We were delegated to collect the Land rent from local farmers. If they cannot pay the rent they can't plow the land. We have the authority to collect rent in few villages. We have a mango orchard each year we have to go

17

collect Mangoes during harvesting season. We use to have a Manager to manage the farm, 6-12 Employees to manage the farm. 20 Oxen to plow the land- 1 Dedicated Herd keeper to take care of the cattle Barn. Twenty cows to have milk & have spare oxes to plow the land with one dedicated herd keeper. We had at least 20-Black buffalos to have enough milk & Ghee – Dedicated herd keeper. Few Extra people to churn the Milk to create Butter or Ghee.

Our land is fertile and can have everything at home. We needed to buy from the market, Salt, Black paper & Kerosene oil.

Introduction of Shri, Prayag Sahu and Shrimati Ramdei Sahun Banka, Garhwa, Bihar

It used to be a big joint family at that time they start separate cooking to control the division of labour, cooking, family affairs but farming was together, but separate management of farming.

He Shri, Prayag Sahu (started his own clothing & lending money business as well as farming. He was very honest working, good to people with good nature, soft spoken, hard-working, very nice gentle man. People still remember him. He was able to get married two daughters in spite of Dorey system. At that time He was handling own finances. Pretty much, lands & collect rent from the village as separated. It was not written or divided on paper.

After the early death of my Father Sri, Prayag Sahu in June 3rd.1947, my whole family was devastated. Out of 6 sisters only two sisters were married. Afterwards, the responsibility came to my mother but with the help of our relatives and uncles we got all daughters married one after the other.4 sisters got married.

We two brothers were the youngest. At that time there was a dowry system- to have a better family you have to offer some money & gifts to entertain the boy's family. My uncle proposed for the division of wealth. He took the major portion of acres of good land. He took almost 300 acres of land, wealth & cash. We have a lending business and cloth business at that time.

DR. BHOLA AND USHA WEDDING

*Shanti Kashyap, Dr. Bhola Kashyap, Dr. Usha Kashyap, Dr. Bharat P. Kashyap –
July 2nd, 1971.*

*Shiv Pd. Kashyap, Dr. Banshi Kashyap, Dr. Bharat Kashyap, Bhikhari Sahu, Shiv
Nath Sahu, Participant in Marriage Ceremony on July 2nd 1971.*

DR. BHOLA AND USHA KASHYAP

DR. BHOLA AND USHA FAMILY

Dr.Banshi Kashyap, Piush Kashyap, Dr.Usha Kashyap, Dr. Bhola Kashyap, Dr. Amit Kashyap, Deborah Kashyap, Domonique Kashyap, Dr. Samir Kashyap

Dr. Bhola Kashyap, Dr.Usha Kashyap with their son – Piush Kashyap's family

Param Kashyap, Piush Kashyap, Dr. Pooja Kashyap, Presha Kashyap

DR. BHOLA AND USHA FAMILY

Domonique Kashyap and Dr. Samir Kashyap's wedding

Deborah Kashyap and Dr. Amit Kashyap

Introduction of Banshi P Kashyap and Bhola Kashyap- Shrimati Ramdei Sahun-Banka

There was Up to 5th grade School in the village school. We went to the same that time too. We have about 200 acres left & one village to collect Land rent. With a manager & sympathetic hard-working employees. Stll we have all the arrangemet same as above with two separate administration. We have to keep one dedicated manager, One- Cashier or Munibjee-to keep track of lending & rent buisnss,6-12 employess to manage the farm, two herd keeper- cows & oxes. One Bullock Cart to carry goods and A good horse-which I use to ride to go to farm along with some assistant. We have enough resources for farming, lending & Clothing business.

My mom managed to get all her daughter's marriages done. We have very good relatives who help in any situation. When my Brother was in elementary school Banka he studied up to 5th grade. Then to Garhwa, stay with My Grandmother (Nani) Bhikha Sahun & Grandpa (Nana Jee} Bhuneshwer Sahu, live & study there. They are also businessmen. He also passed away. He has a son, Mathura Sahu, his wife passed away at an early age, no kids. My grandmother was a very good-hearted Lady, she took care of my brother very well. Since we have a big farm each week essential things send from the farm with an employee working on the farm.

Even one cow kept there so no scarcity of milk. We have one Bullock cart that used to go shopping every week since it was the nearest shopping place within six miles. After grade one to 5th Grade at Village, they open up to 7th Grade in Banka. Since I was the youngest child, my mom said *"You study at home after 7ᵗʰ Grade, you go to Garhwa"*. In 8th Grade, I was enrolled in Govind High School Garhwa after 7th grade, Jharkhand. When my brother completed 5th Grade in 1955, he went to Garhwa. Banshi Kashyap enrolled in Swami Dayanand Arya-vedic Middle School. He Completed 7th Grade in 1957 He enrolled in Govind High School Garhwa. 1962 and graduated from high school.

While he was in high school got Married in march 1960 with Smt. Prema Kashyap Daughter of Sri Ram Chandra Prasad & Smt Dharma Devi, Dehri On Sone, Rohtash. Since all the sisters got married no one was at home with Mom. In spite of disagreement, he was enrolled in Saint-Xaviers College Ranchi. He wanted to be an Engineer but he changed his mind and started preparing for Pre-med & change major in biology geared towards Medical College. Bihar Now Jharkhand. New Medical College -Rajendra Medical College Ranchi, started in the same year. He enrolled in the 2ⁿᵈ batch of Medical School Ranchi-Rajendra Medical College Ranchi. After the initial requirement, he enrolled in Rajendra Medical College in Ranchi, Jharkhand in 1964 and graduated in 1970.

I continue to study in Garhwa. In the meantime, we purchased a house in Garhwa in 1960, near my grandfather's (Nana Jee) House. We Paid Cash at that time.

My Mother getting lonely at home to have some Company My brother got married when he was in high school in March 1960. Out of marriage:

DR. BANSHI KASHYAP FAMILY

Dr. Banshi and Prema Kashyap

Dr. Bhola & Usha Kashyap,
Dr. Banshi & Prema Kashyap

Aryan Kashyap, Neela Kashyap,
Aman Kashyap

Rijul Kashyap, Megha & Vijay Kashyap

DR. BANSHI KASHYAP FAMILY

Neela Kashyap, Prema Kashyap,
Megha Kashyap, Dr. Banshi Kashyap,
Vijay Kashyap, Jitendra Kashyap

Sunita & Nishit Parikh

First Row, Prema, Dr. Banshi, Sunita,
Lalita, Nandita - (Dr. Banshi Family) Standing

Nandita Mehra, Sunita Parikh,
Lalita, Yadhav, Vijay Kashyap,
Jitendra Kashyap

NANDITA AND MANISH MEHRA FAMILY

ALL THE GRAND KIDS OF DR. BHOLA AND DR. BANSHI KASHYAP

Ishan, Parma, Prashant, Anjali, Anneya, Aryan, Aman.

Introduction of Dr. Banshi p Kashyap & Prema Kashyap Daughter of Shri Ram Chnder Prasad and Shri Mati Dharma Devi-Dehi-on-Sone, Rohtash, Bihar.

Banshi Prasad Kashyap and Prema Kashyap, have the following Children all Born in Banka.

Daughters: 3

1. Sunita Kashyap's first daughter born in 1962 Banka
2. Lalita Kashyap
3. Nandita Kashyap

Sons: 2

1. Vijay Kashyap
2. Jitendra Kashyap was born when he left for the USA.

All Born in Banka, Jharkhand, India.

Present all in USA are two sons:

Introduction of Vijay Kashyap
and Megha Kashyap

Vijay Kashyap and wife Megha Kashyap-
Married in Nagpur,India.
Vijay Kashyap-MS- IT Manager-CA, Wife-Megha Kashyap

Son: 1
1. Rijul Kashyap

Introduction of Jitendra Kashyap -Neela Kashyap

Jitendra Kashyap-MS-Artitecht Wife-
Neela Kashyap-MS-Artitecht
Married in Goregau-Mumbai, India.

Sons: 2
1. Aryan Kashyap-MS Artitech(St)
2. Aman Kashyap

Introduction of Sunita Parikh -Nishit Parikh married in Mumbai, living in KS. Sunita Parikh married to Nishit Parikh- MS (chemical)/Business Man

Son:1
1. Ishan Parikh-MS-Director Arts & Movie

Daughter:
1. Tanvi Parikh-Pharmacist Married to Hasan
2. Niralee Parikh

Introduction of Lalita Yadhav and Sanjeev Yadhav

Lalita Yadhav- Married to Sanjeev Yadhav, Married in Andheri-Mumbai-living in Reston Verginia.

Daughters- 2
1. Aishwarya Yadhav-Medical Std.
2. Ruma Yadhav-Medical Std.

Introduction of Nandita Mehra And Manish Mehra

Married in Kernal-India, Lives in CA. Nandita Mehra- Pharmacist - married to Manish Mehra-MS- Business

Son:1
1. Rahul Mehra-MS-Business

Daughter:2
1. Anjali Mehra-Medical-Std.
2. Aaniya Mehra

Introduction of Dr. Bhola Prasad Kashyap, alias Sita Ram Sahu, and Dr. Usha Rani Kashyap Married in Ranchi, July 2nd 1971.

Bhola P. Kashyap-Usha R. Kashyap had 3 sons, 1 daughter.

Introduction of Piush and Pooja Kashyap

Piush Kashyap- Born in Ranchi- Dec. 21st 1973- MS-IT Manager/Business Owner married to Pooja Kashyap MD- Pediatric -Cardiologist-Delhi India, lives in San Antonio Texas. Daughter of Mr. Satish Khurana and MS, Kiran Khurana.

Daughter:1
1. Presha Kashyap

Son:1
1. Param Kashyap

Introduction of Amit Kashyap and Deborah Kashyap

Amit Kashyap-MD (Family Practice-Internal Medicine Born in Ranchi-Dec.8th, 1979, married to Deborah Kashyap-Attorney at law- Kansas.

Introduction of Dr. Samir Kashyap and Domoniue Kashyap

Dr. Samir Kashyap- Neuro-vascular-Surgeon-CA. Born in USA-KS-Dec.13th,1987 Married to Domoniue Kashyap -Attorney at Law-CA,on April 20th.2024.CA.Lives in Fresno-CA.

DR. BHOLA AND USHA FAMILY GARHWA JHARKHAND EYE CLINIC

Dr. Banshi Kashyap

Eye Clinic - Garhwa Jharkhand House Picture

DR. BANSHI KASHYAP & BHOLA KASHYAP FAMILY

Vhawan (friend of Nandita), Sunita Kashyap, Nandita Kashyap, Bhola Kashyap, Usha Kashyap, Megha Kashyap, Vijay Kashyap

Vijay Kashyap, Megha Kashyap, Rijul Kashyap

Vhawan (friend of Nandita), Sunita Kashyap, Nandita Kashyap, Bhola Kashyap, Usha Kashyap, Megha Kashyap, Vijay Kashya

After the Marriage, my responsibility increased. If anything happened I had to go home & take care of farming responsibilities to see everything going smoothly. My sister & brother in law's family were very cooperative anything happened I had to go to their home to accompany & bring them home. Anybody marriage, any religious function, I had to attend since my brother studying out of town.

When I graduated from high school, I enrolled in Ranchi College Ranchi. 1968-69. I got admitted in MGM Medical College Jamshedpur1969-70. Whenever I get a chance I have to travel to Garhwa, Banka to take care of domestic affairs. At that time older daughter Sunita start studying in Girls Middle School Garhwa. One of our youngest Sister's family stays with us. We supported their expenses. Since there was an abundance produce at home, nothing to worry about eating & drink. There was no modern houses but we had an abundance of love & care for one another in the family.

When my brother got graduated from Medical school in in 1970. While he was finishing his internship, he got a Job offer with a green card from the USA. He was debating what to do? My mother was against it but with his persuasion, mother got agreed. My father-in-law, Bhart Pd, Kashyap and Shanti Kashyap. The house was near my Nani's house. He offered to get married to his daughter Usha Rani Kashyap and agreed. I accepted to get married to Usha R. Kashyap for two reasons:

1. *Loan obligation taken during Education.*
2. *My brother wanted to come to USA expenses obligation.*

There was a dowry system at that time. We needed some resources to continue the education of two people. It was an unpleasant feeling. I was getting a lot of offers to get married with nine different girl's families. My father-in-law from Garhwa was working at Rajendra Medical College Ranchi a lecturer in Eye Department Ranchi and other relative. He offered our family to give support & gift to get married to me. With his persuasion & mother's decision decided to get married before *Dr. Banshi Kashyap* (My brother) left for USA. I got married to *Usha R Kashyap(She was in High School)*, Daughter of *Dr. Bharat P Kashyap & Shanti Kashyap* Ranchi, Jharkhand in July 2nd, 1971. In December 1971, he (Dr.Banshi P Kashyap) left for the USA. We were very deserted after he left. I continued my study in MGM Medical College. It was tough for me to take care of his kids & home front. With the help of relative dedicated staff at home, things continued to be running. During this phase, we have to sell some land to continue education and home front. He passed his ECFMG in the first year then started his Residency in New York City. Once he finished residency, he visited India to visit family, initially he was ready to take boys only, but mom said it would be better to have all the family together. When joined a fellowship in KU Medical Center and then moved to Kansas & all family members joined in 1977. I had to take care of Immigration & Passport for Six People, it was not that easy but get it done.

I graduated from medical school in 1976. After finishing I did advanced training & education in Opthalmology. I joined Nehru Institute of Ophthalmology Sitapur under Lucknow University. My wife was studying at Rajendra Medical College

Ranchi. In the mean time I as working at District Hospital Giridih, Jharkhand. I was in charge of District Hospital Bihar Government- Civil Assistant surgeon. Furthermore, I got transferred at the Garhwa District Eye Department to take care of Meral Hospital & Banka Health Center. My practice is based in Garhwa, Bihar now Jharkhand. After Graduation, my wife did a residency in OB/GYNs. She did residency in ophthalmology. She was awarded a Hons in Anatomy. While she was in Medical School she gave Birth to *Piush Kashyap* in Dec. 23rd, 1973 Ranchi.- Present MS- Manager IT/business owner: Wife – *Pooja Kashyap* M.D., Present Pediatrics –Cardiologist. Her Father is *Satish Khurana* & Wife is Mrs. *Kiran Khurana*. Two grandchildren - *Presha Kashyap and Param Kashyap.*

Amit kashyap Dec. 8th 1979 Ranchi-Present MD-Internal Medicine: Wife - *Deborah Kashyap* Attorney at law.

Samir Kashyap Dec. 13th 1987, KS-USA: Wife - *Domonique Kashyap*. Married to Samir April 20th 2024. Samir Kashyap is a Neurosurgeon in CA, his Wife is Attorney at law.

I was settled in India with good Job & Practice but He (Dr. Banshi P Kashyap) wanted to see all the family and mom together. He encouraged to apply for a Visa by that time immigration rules were modified but in no time our immigration got approved. All of God's Plan and his persuasion and my father-in-law's (Dr. Bharat P Kashyap) encouragement led to the decision to immigrate in 1981 Nov to Kansas City Overland Park.

Worked with three eye surgeon groups for two years they gave sponsoring support for my family then they joined in 1983

Usha, Piush, Amit and Nanhe jee(Surendra Kashyap Usha's brother got admitted to FIT Florida) After a few years we worked in Health Care. Since Medical licensing was getting tougher. We didn't pass the Board.

Once Usha settled in Kansas, we all did healthcare Jobs to support the family. We continue to strive & support to better off family. My brother is still backup support. We became Respiratory Care practitioners to support ourselves & Family. When Usha became a Citizen she sponsored her mom to come to the USA. By that time Surendra Kashyap got married in India with Poonam Kashyap.

DR. BHARAT KASHYAP & SHANTI KASHYAP FAMILY

Dr. Bharat Kashyap & Shanti Kashyap

Dr. Bharti & Dr. Birendra Kashyap

Shanti, Poonam, and Surendra kashyap

DR. BHARAT KASHYAP & SHANTI KASHYAP FAMILY

Dr. Bharti, Dr. Birendra,
Standing - Dr. Bibhuti, Dr. Nidhi, Dr. Nimesh Kashyap

Vibha, Osho Viraj, Nimisha, Rajesh Gupta - Top
Vien, Neev, Nimesha, Nilesh, Reyansh, Osho - Bottom

DR. BHARAT KASHYAP & SHANTI KASHYAP FAMILY

Aanan Kashyap, Shanti Kashyap, Shaan Kashyap, Dr. Ravindra Kashyap,
Sarah Kashyap

Adish, Shant, Dishan - Lower
Aditi, Narendra Kashyap – Upper

DR. BHARAT KASHYAP & SHANTI KASHYAP FAMILY

Pooja Kashyap, Shanti, Brian

Narendra, Shanti, Aditi

DR. BHARAT KASHYAP & SHANTI KASHYAP FAMILY

Introduction of Dr.Bharat P. Kashyap and Mrs. Shanti Kashyap-Ranchi

Dr. Bharat P Kashyap Prof. RMC Ophalmology: Wife (Mother-in-law) Shanti Kashyap

Daughters:2
1. Dr.Usha R, Kashyap Married to Dr. Bhola P Kashyap, MD, DOMS,
2. Viva R, Kashyap-MS-IT Married to Rajesh Gupta-MS-Civil-Gorakhpur-Ranchi,India.

They have two Daughters.

Viva Rani Kashyap and Rajesh Gupta

Daughter:2
1. Nimisha Gupta-MS-IT-Married to Biren Gupta-
MS-IT Manager, from Delhi.Their Children

Son:1
Neev Gupta
Daughter:1
Vaani Gupta

2. Anusha Gupta-MS-It Married to Nilesh
Lulle-MS -IT, Banglore, India.They have one Child:

Son:1
Reyansh Lulle

1. *Surendra Kashyap*- MS-IT Manager/Invester, Married to Mrs Poonam Kashyap-MS-IT-Manager-From Pune-India.

2. *Birendra Kashyap* MS-Eye Surgeon Ranchi: Wife - *Bharti Kashyap* MS-Eye Surgeon Ranchi, India.

3. *Vibha Rani Gupta* MS-IT - Married to *Rajesh Gupta* MS-Civil, Gorakhpur, Ranchi, India.

4. *Ravindra Kashyap* MD. Passed ECFMG from Thailand, and joined after Smt., *Shanti Kashyap, He had the opportunity to get married in India but He married Sarah Kashyap, RN, During Residency-She is from the Philippines.*

5. Narendra Kashyap - Naval Engineer & *Aditi* was on the ship. They decided to join in the USA.

Introduction of Surendra Kasyap and Poonam Kashyap

Surendra Kashyap MS-IT Manager/Investor:
Wife- *Poonam Kashyap* MS-IT Manager. They
had three Children born in the USA:

Sons-2
1. *Alake Kashyap- MS-Tax, Married to Yogi Kashyap MD*
   Have two children
   Son-1 Nalin Kashyap
   Daughter-1.Meera Kashyap

2. *Dr. Sarang Kashyap-Pulmonary -Critical Care, Married*
   to Dr.Nikki Kashyap-Anesthesia. Have one daughter
   1. Mila Kashyap

Daughter-1
1. *Pooja Kashyap- MS-Artitecht, Marred to Brian- MS -Artiteccht*

Introduction of Dr. Birendra Kashyap-MS- Eye Surgeon, Married to Dr. Bharti Kashyap-MS-Eye Surgeon- from Patna, lives in Ranchi.

Birendra Kashyap and Bharti Kasyap-They have two sons.

Sons:2
1. Dr.Bibhuti Kashyap-Eye Surgeon, Married to Dr.Nidhi Kashyap-MS-Eye Surgeon Ranchi.
2. Dr.Nimesh Kashyap-MBBS.

Introduction to Narendra Kashyap- MS-IT/ Naval Engineer and Aditi Kashyap- MA

Aditi from Patna lives in Columbus Ohio. She is the best person to keep all family together. My Mother inlaw likes to live with her.Both husband & wife very nice for everyone. They have two boys:

Sons-2
1. *Adhish Kashyap-Medical St.*
2. *Dishan Kashyap -College St.*

Introduction of Dr. Ravindra Kashyap MD, Pulmonary Critical Care Married to Mrs, Sarah Kashyap RN, They live in Peoria, IL. They have two Sons;

Sons:-2

1. *Aanan Kashyap- BS*
2. *Shaan Kashyap- College st.*

All worked hard to achieve their Goal in the USA.

Dr. Banshi P Kashyap MD, FACP, came in 1971.He was born on September 15th. 1944 in Banka India passed away on March 2nd 2024 in Las Vegas. Chief of Staff at VA Hospital Las Vegas NV. He took the courage to come and establish himself in USA, out of all adversity in this country. we all follow after he arrives in the USA. God loves him, he is in our hearts.

OUR BIG KASHYAP FAMILY

DR. BHARAT AND SHANTI'S BIG FAMILY

KASHYAP BIG FAMILY

We are the creation of beliefs and success. Any area of your life is a direct result of your belief system. To change anything in life, the one thing that you need to do is to change your beliefs – then your beliefs will become reality by utilizing the four laws of success. The law of belief, the law of expectation, the law of imagination, the law of attraction.

Dr.Bhola P. Kashyap , MD, DOMS, MBA - Eye Surgeon and Business Owner. He's been helping people all over the world become a better person. Dr.Bhola & Usha Kashyap have three sons. They also have two grandchildren. Dr. Bhola was Inspired to write a book about family history. Hence, this book is all about his personal as well as his extended family's achievement!

To my Wife, Usha, Life has been worthwhile with you,

Sincerely, Bhola